Shifted: A 14-Day Journey of Release and Renewal

By: Federica Robinson-Bryant, PhD

Preface by the late Rev. Dr. Micheal J. Robinson, Sr.

Shifted: A 14-Day Journey of Release and Renewal

Published by Denotion Research Group
www.DenotionResearch.com

ISBN:
978-1-958634-31-8 (Paperback)
978-1-958634-32-5 (eBook)

Printed in United States 1st Edition

To every soul bravely pursuing their transformation: may this book be a companion on your journey. Embrace the exploration of your past, gently release the burdens of pain, and rise, renewed and transformed. May you discover the strength within to shift toward a future filled with hope and purpose.

Contents

His Letter,
Early 2000s

Daddy

Rev. Dr. Micheal
J. Robinson, Sr.

Preface

Outlook on Your Future

Who am I?

Ask if you must, this is what I have to say.

I shall say unto you that I am the light that illuminates the answer as to everything that you are looking for and that you need to know. Guess what, I've got it all.

The bottom line is that as a student or child you don't know yourself. What do you know? School and or life has to be about more than memories and memorizing what other people have done or playing it safe. It's about learning to find your own greatness. Greatness is always within each of us.

Fix your mind on the things you can conceive because if it can be conceived, it can also be achieved. Look out with your imagination to find out where you have been and where you are going. Sometimes a lot of what you're looking for is missed because you're too busy overlooking what's real for what is just a dream or what's not right for you.

Choices

Someday life is going to be about making choices. Making the right choice to stay in school, to become the best that you can be, with the dream of succeeding to the highest level of your dreams. Your future is the beginning of what you do today. So, today, choose how high you want to go in the future that you seek. To do nothing is a waste of a beautiful mind that has nothing but unlimited heights.

Don't hold back. I want you to give it all that you've got. The reason is, as a parent I ask for your all because unless you give it all you've got, you are not pressing your way into your dreams. Then I have failed to help you to achieve your greatness, your goal, meaning only that you must succeed in order for me not to fail.

Lay your heart in a place that only you can break. Meaning, make the right choices as no one can stop your dreams but you. No matter what they say or do, they cannot harm your dreams.

Dream on to success. Peace be still and collect all the knowledge that you can store within you. One day you will see that the choice you made was the right choice.

When everyone said she will never mount to anything, you say to them that the days, months, and years have passed but not once did you give up on your dreams. Ask them to think back on the times when they thought you were crazy or weird. Let them all now see what your dreams were all about. Your love for learning at its highest level has now taken you to the place where others may only dream about. Thank God for his giving and what he gave to you. With love and total happiness, I shall forever be with you. If you will please place me in your heart for I am with you.

Dream the realities of the future,

Day 1

An Inward Journey

I've been circling this moment, this act of creation, for what feels like an eternity. The blank page, the blinking cursor, the weight of untold stories – they've haunted me, beckoned me, then watched me retreat, time and time again. I've been a master of distraction, a virtuoso of de-prioritization. I've shifted focus like a restless spirit, changed the angle of my narrative until it was unrecognizable, rewritten the structure and contents so many times that the original intent was lost in the convolution of revisions. But, as the saying goes, "just do it." And so, here I am, finally, unequivocally, "this is it."

This isn't just another attempt, another fleeting impulse. This is a declaration, a commitment to excavate emotions, to lay bare the landscape of my soul. And as I embark on this journey, I want to make one thing irrefutably clear: this is my story, and mine alone. I have no intention of dragging anyone else into the shadows of my past. I am striving to craft a narrative that is both honest and self-contained, a testament to my own experiences, my own transformations. I've learned that the only way to emerge from this process with my integrity intact is to own my truth, to speak my truth, and to leave others to their own. I am no longer consumed by anger, no longer shackled by blame. I am simply weary, a weariness that has settled deep within my bones, a weariness that demands release, that compels me to move forward.

And yes, I am aware of my tendencies. I am prone to digressions, to meandering narratives, to the chaotic beauty of "beating bushes and driving down long dirt roads and wading in the water." So, I ask for your patience, your understanding, as I navigate the entanglement of my own thoughts and experiences.

This book is more than just a memoir; it's an act of liberation. I have lived behind a barricade of unconscious facades and rebellions, attempting to appease identities that have long since abandoned me. This charade has yielded a darkening, an unease, a sense of being lost in a world I thought I once understood. I have used people, responsibilities, and the relentless pursuit of external validation, as a means of avoidance, a way to cloud the question of who I truly was, who I truly sought to be.

I was once defined by a series of roles: 24/7 mother, wife, daughter, professor, professional, Christian. These were the pillars of my identity, the markers of my place in the world. But those pillars have crumbled, leaving behind a landscape of brokenness, pain, dissociation, and profound loneliness.

Now, I stand at a crossroads, facing the daunting task of defining who I aim to be.

Before I can even begin to envision who I aim to become, I must first answer a more profound question: who am I, really? Not the person I was told to be, or the person I pretended to be, but the person I am at my essence. This deeper understanding is the key to unlocking my potential for transformation.

Ultimately, I yearn to be "Shifted," a being transformed, a spirit reborn. This book is my web of self-discovery, a journey to reclaim my authentic self, to cultivate self-love, and to find balance in the chaos of daily life. I grapple with the urge to restart, to erase the past and begin anew. But I am learning to embrace the concept of pivoting, of building upon the foundation of my experiences, of discovering a new version of myself, a version I have yet to fully know. Welcome to the unfolding. Welcome to my shift.

Dare to Be Free

I dare to be free.

Unleash the me I couldn't see.

To break the lens once blurred by buried dreams.

Drowned by a lifetime of trauma and self-inflicted depletes.

I dare to be free.

To unapologetically pour my love upon me.

Rather than freely give to those without the capacity to receive.

*To embrace the richness that has been suppressed by sacrifice
and silent screams.*

Day 2

The Prophecy of Greatness

I once heard a short, but quite significant story.

A whisper from the past, a seed planted in the fertile ground of my nascent existence, a promise that has echoed through the corridors of my life: "She will do great things." It's a simple phrase, yet it has been the compass guiding my journey, the north star illuminating my path.

My parents, in their infinite wisdom, shared the story of my arrival, a narrative steeped with divine intervention. My mother, a young military wife yearning for a child, found herself in a small-town revival, a place where faith and hope intertwined. There, a visiting prophet, her voice resonating with an otherworldly authority, called her forth, declaring her pregnant with a daughter, a child destined for greatness. That child, of course, was me.

From that moment, the prophecy became a part of my identity, a silent companion, a constant reminder of my potential. I clung to the idea that I would one day fulfill this destiny, that I would somehow recognize the moment my mission was complete. But what, precisely, constituted "greatness"? The word itself is subjective, a nebulous concept that shifts and changes with perspective. Yet, as I probed further, as I examined the core of my being, I realized that my mission was not so elusive.

Greatness, I determined, was not about grand gestures or public accolades. It was about living authentically, thriving on my own terms, embracing the fullness of my being. It was about being a conduit of blessings, leveraging my gifts to uplift and empower others. It was about fostering genuine connection, loving and being loved in return. It was about sowing seeds of hope, inspiration, and inner abundance, contributing to the betterment of our shared world.

Armed with these ideals, I navigated the complexities of life, acknowledging my human fallibility, my moments of imperfection. Like any other soul, I have stumbled, I have erred, I have made choices that, in hindsight, I might have altered. But I have always strived to live passionately, knowing that my purpose, my divine mandate, was yet to be fully realized.

There was a period, however, a brief but significant interlude, when I strayed from the path, when I questioned the very foundation of my beliefs. In the crucible of adolescence, as I wrestled with the seeming contradictions between science and religion, creationism and evolution, I found myself adrift. Perhaps it was a rebellious phase, a desire to assert my independence, a struggle to reconcile the teachings of my pastor father with the burgeoning logic of my own mind. Whatever the cause, I declared myself an atheist, a defiant act of intellectual rebellion.

Yet, the emptiness that followed was palpable. The absence of faith left a void, a sense of disorientation. As the child of a prophecy, I had been gifted with a toolkit, a set of spiritual and psychological tools that grounded me, that provided direction and purpose. How could I forsake the divine gift I'd received?

This "toolkit," or perhaps, as I now see it, "God's armor," consisted of Inspiration and Hope, Guidance and Direction, Cultural and Religious Influence, Political and Social Impact, and Psychological Impact.

With Inspiration and Hope

"She will do great things" whispered a promise of purpose into the deepest recesses of my soul. Though the specifics of my destined greatness remained veiled in mystery, an ethereal vision of positive change and profound influence ignited an unyielding flame within me. Even when doubt threatened to extinguish it, that unwavering belief in my potential fueled my resilience, urging me to rise again and again, to keep striving, to keep believing that something extraordinary awaited me. It was a light in the darkness, a gentle reminder that my journey held significance, even when the path ahead seemed unclear.

With Guidance and Direction

"She will do great things" became an internal compass, guiding my decision-making processes through the maze of life's choices. While some paths were clearly marked with warning signs, others were masked in ambiguity, their consequences obscured. Yet, the prophecy served as a steady hand, a guiding light, reminding me that the direction was always forward, always toward growth, always toward fulfilling my potential. It was a quiet assurance that even amidst uncertainty, there was a purpose, a direction, a reason to keep moving, to keep progressing.

With Cultural and Religious Influence

"She will do great things" shaped the very fabric of my being, molding me into a better human, a more compassionate and understanding soul. It instilled within me a deep-seated respect for the diversity of human experience, shaping my beliefs, values, and traditions. It nurtured a fervent desire to celebrate the unique beauty and inherent worth of every individual, to embrace the richness of our shared humanity. It was a constant reminder that greatness was not just about personal achievement, but about contributing to the betterment of the world around me.

With Political and Social Impact

"She will do great things" resonated within me, fueling a profound passion for political and social justice. It ignited a love for humanity in all its diverse forms, transcending the boundaries of race, class, and social status. It fostered a deep respect for differences, a yearning for a world where peaceful coexistence was not just a dream, but a lived reality. It was a call to action, a reminder that my voice mattered, that my actions could contribute to creating a more just and equitable world for all.

With Psychological Impact

"She will do great things" became a shield against fear, a source of faith. It instilled a sense of invulnerability, a belief that my life was protected, that my purpose was yet to be fulfilled. This belief, however naive, provided a sense of comfort in the face of danger, a feeling that I was somehow destined to survive, to overcome, to fulfill the prophecy. It was a psychological anchor, a source of strength in moments of vulnerability, a reminder that my story was not yet complete.

Armed with this armor, the greatest gift my parents could have given me, I have journeyed through life, sometimes walking, sometimes waltzing, sometimes sprinting, and sometimes running. I have stumbled, I have fallen, but I have always risen, guided by the echo of the prophecy, the promise of greatness, the unwavering belief that my purpose is yet to be fulfilled.

Destiny's Call

A prophet proclaimed in a single breath,
"She will do great things".
This guides a heart and instills great hope,
Revealing a burning flame.

Where strength is forged, and truths are sowed,
A hidden grace, now brought to light,
Spirit's journey, endures all things,
While His Will takes its flight.

Through shadowed valleys, and eerie spaces,
Thus, seeking a brighter day.
The prophecy's echo, continues to sound,
as she steadily finds her way.

To heal the wounds, and stem the tide.
A vessel filled, with purpose deep,
To ultimately answer Destiny's call.
To plant her hope, where shadows sleep.

Day 3

A Shepherd's Twisted Tale

The age-old metaphor of sheep, lamb, and wolf tempts us to simplify the human experience, to categorize ourselves and others into easily understood boxes. Yet, the truth is far more nuanced. Within each of us resides a complex interplay of these archetypes, a constant push and pull between conformity, compassion, and raw, untamed strength. What I've learned is that life is not a linear progression from one state to another, but a swirling vortex of emotions and experiences, a dance of adaptation and resilience. It's in the recognition of this fluidity, this constant negotiation between our inner sheep, lamb, and wolf, that we begin to truly understand the intricate nature of our own being.

This understanding was solidified during a thought-provoking conversation with a Haitian male colleague, a moment of spiritual resonance that challenged my preconceived notions. He presented a direct question: if you could only be one, which would it be? I found myself unable to choose. Why settle for the limitations of these singular identities? In that moment, I asserted that I wasn't meant to be confined to just one of these creatures. I was meant to embody them all, to navigate the intricacies of life with the wisdom of the wolf, the compassion of the lamb, and the adaptability of the sheep.

Thus, in the metaphorical landscape of my life, these three terms represent not rigid categories, but dynamic aspects of my journey. However, the timing of their evocation matters immensely. I can vividly recall moments when I instinctively acted as a sheep, when the assertive strength of the wolf would have served me better. Conversely, there were times when my compassionate lamb nature emerged, while the adaptable pragmatism of the sheep would have yielded more effective results. Whether those choices were ultimately beneficial or detrimental, each instance of inhabiting these different 'skins' has proven crucial to my ongoing process of self-discovery. Each instance offers a vital clue in understanding the minutiae of my personality, and that lessons learned are invaluable as I continue to navigate the complexities of life.

Federica, The Sheep

This archetype embodies the societal pressures, the expectations, the subtle and overt demands to conform. It represents the moments when I've felt compelled to follow the herd, to suppress my individuality, to submit, and to adhere to predetermined roles.

For instance, when I was a new faculty member, I felt immense pressure to conform to the established norms of academia. Being hired alongside another Black woman, we constituted the only Black women in the College faculty and the only women in our engineering department. This added layer of visibility and scrutiny amplified the pressure to fit in. To many, she and I were the same person, names used interchangeably. I found myself suppressing my innovative teaching methods and research interests, instead adhering to the expectations of my department. I diligently attended committee meetings, volunteered for extra work, and consciously muted my voice in many rooms. I was acting as the sheep, following the well-worn path, prioritizing conformity and submission over my own creative and intellectual instincts, in an attempt to gain acceptance and avoid rocking the boat. One wonders what I could have accomplished, had I fully embraced the wolf in my work.

Beyond the professional sphere, another stark example of conforming to the sheep archetype occurred during my college years. I recall calling a boyfriend, asking him to visit so we could have a serious conversation about a complication he had seemingly caused. He arrived, and after the conversation, he forcibly engaged in nonconsensual, anal sex. I curled up, my body shaking with silent sobs, and cried, the tears a cold, heavy weight, marking the beginning of a shift, a change I knew I could never undo. It was a moment of utter submission, a stark manifestation of the 'sheep' archetype, where I silenced my own voice and surrendered to an act of profound violation.

Federica, The Lamb

This embodies my capacity for empathy, compassion, and vulnerability. It represents the nurturing side of my nature, the innate desire to connect, to heal, to offer solace.

When I took on the role of homeschooling my four children during the pandemic, becoming their sole educator, their emotional anchor, their near everything, I was embracing the lamb in its purest form. The world had descended into chaos, and my children, like so many others, were grappling with fear, uncertainty, and the sudden disruption of their routines. I knew I had competing responsibilities, like my work-from-home professorship, which demanded my attention and focus. But the needs of my children took precedence. I poured every ounce of my energy into nurturing their minds and spirits, creating a safe haven within the confines of our home. It was an act of love, a testament to the power of empathy, and a profound expression of the lamb within me.

Another example of embodying the lamb arose in my interactions with my students. Beyond the formal role of professor, I often found myself acting as a mentor and confidante. Recognizing the pressures and anxieties my students faced, both academically and personally, I made myself available to listen, to offer guidance, and to provide encouragement. I would spend extra time explaining complex concepts, not just intellectually, but also emotionally, understanding that their ability to learn was often intertwined with their well-being. I created a safe space in my classroom and online office, where students felt comfortable sharing their struggles and seeking support. I was the lamb, offering a nurturing presence, fostering a sense of belonging, and extending compassion beyond the boundaries of traditional academic expectations.

Federica, The Wolf

This signifies my inner strength, my resilience, and my untamed spirit. It represents the moments when I've asserted my independence, challenged the status quo, and broken free from the constraints of societal expectations.

When I chose to accept the inevitable end of my marriage and forge a new path as a single parent, I was unleashing the wolf within, a primal force I had long suppressed. It wasn't a decision made lightly, nor without profound fear. I knew I was stepping into a period of immense financial burden, facing the daunting reality of limited day-to-day support, and bracing for the inherently imbalanced demands of single parenting. Yet, beneath the terror and uncertainty, a fierce determination began to surface. I will not simply survive; I will thrive. I will build a life on my own terms, a testament to my resilience, my strength, and the untamed spirit of the wolf that had finally been unleashed.

Another instance where I embrace the wolf is in my ongoing advocacy for diversity, equity, and inclusion despite the current social and political climate. I refuse to be a passive observer of systemic biases and discriminatory practices as I continuously learn more about the world. I now challenge systems, voice my concerns, assemble teams, and actively work to create a more inclusive and equitable environment. I organize workshops, mentor underrepresented individuals, and push for policy changes that address the root causes of inequality. I am the wolf, challenging the established power structures, asserting my voice, and fighting for a more just and equitable community, even when faced with resistance and opposition.

The key, I've discovered, is not to rigidly compartmentalize these archetypes as inherently good or bad, but to recognize their context-dependent utility. It's about cultivating the wisdom to recognize when to embrace the sheep's adaptability, seamlessly blending into the environment to navigate complex social structures. It's about knowing when to extend the lamb's unwavering compassion, offering solace and support to those in need, and to myself. And it's about possessing the courage to unleash the wolf's fierce independence, to challenge injustice, to defend boundaries, and to pursue one's authentic path with conviction. These aspects are not mutually exclusive, but rather, interconnected facets of my complex identity, each enriching and informing the others.

The shepherd's twisted tale, then, is not a narrative of rigid choices, of selecting a singular path, a fixed identity, a static archetype. It's a journey of embracing the inherent fluidity of human experience, the intricate web of our inner selves. It's a recognition that we are all capable of embodying the sheep's adaptability, the lamb's empathy, and the wolf's resilience, seamlessly transitioning between these states as circumstances demand. The true journey, the essence of being human, lies in navigating the delicate balance between these powerful forces, in understanding that strength is not about dominance, but about adaptability, that compassion is not weakness, but a profound form of power, and that true independence is not isolation, but a conscious choice to live authentically. It's about recognizing that these archetypes exist within us all, and the mastery of self lies in the ability to access the right one, at the right time. It is a constant, evolving process of self-awareness, self-acceptance, and ultimately, self-mastery.

A Twisted Tale

Oh, twisted tale, a winding road she treads,

By spirit, she rise, where strength is bred.

Stories blend, like rivers flowing free,

A journey's path, to its own destiny.

No single face, can meet each passing hour,

To master, knowing when, to wield a different power.

Like sheep's timid steps, through depths of fear and dread,

Wolf's prowling hunt, where buried wounds are fed.

Lamb's tender spirit, a flame against the chill,

Where life endures, and shadows lose their will.

Not so simple choices, no clear ways to see,

But shifting circumstance, sets her spirit free.

Through trials faced, and lessons learned,

The unraveled shepherd's tale, a state the heart yearns.

Converging paths, where weary souls may roam,

Context undoubtedly calling, to reset the tone.

Day 4

Raised in A Web of Failed Systems

I don't think I've mentioned this yet, but I am a systems engineer. I think deeply about how things are linked together, how parts become whole, and how cause and effects ripple across time. I can't help it; it's an innate perspective, a lens through which I perceive the world – a superpower, perhaps, or a deeply ingrained dysfunction, depending on the day.

Because of this, this reflection ventures into the intricate, often painful, web of my childhood, a landscape I now understand as a series of failed systems. There's a vastness to my experiences, rich with trauma and resilience, and to paint the full picture would be an undertaking far beyond the scope of this chapter. So, I've distilled it, condensed it, striving for a balance between conciseness and raw honesty, though I fear it may still lean towards TMI.

Trauma Abound

Growing up in a rural community, the veil of innocence is often thin, and the whispers of hardship carry far. My grandparents were foster parents, my parents followed suit, and my friends shared their own, often harrowing, experiences. Conversations overheard, phone calls filled with tales of heinous acts – a constant barrage of stories that seeped into my consciousness, shaping my worldview. This exposure, while perhaps a form of grim preparation, instilled a deep-seated fear, a sense that danger lurked in the most unexpected places.

The stories were not abstract; they were visceral. Friends confided in me, revealing the abuse they endured at the hands of those they should have trusted – grandfathers, babysitters, fathers, family friends, cousins, aunts, uncles, siblings. A pervasive sense of distrust settled within me, a distrust that initially targeted men but eventually expanded to encompass all people. I saw that vulnerability was a dangerous game, that anyone could be a perpetrator. I vividly recall a foster child who joined our family, his body bearing the physical scars of repeated abuse, his inability to control his bowels a stark testament to the violation he had endured. That same child, years later, became a perpetrator himself, a tragic illustration of how broken systems perpetuate cycles of pain. Yet, even in his actions, I found a flicker of empathy, a recognition that the outcomes we witness are often the products of deeply flawed systems.

This pattern of brokenness, of systemic failure, extended far beyond the confines of my home and community. It permeated the very institutions meant to protect and guide me. The systems meant to nurture and guide me were, from an early age, a source of both bewilderment and profound distrust. I endured a police officer's predatory calls to my home during high school, a chilling violation masked as a perverse joke offering to "drink my bath water", and fended off the unwanted advances of grown men who sought to exploit my vulnerable, underage form.

In elementary school, my physical education teacher, in front of the entire class, delivered a cruel and baseless prophecy: that I, a consistently high-achieving student that had a tendency to speak her mind, would be dead by the age of twelve. The sheer malice of his words, directed at a child, still echoes in my memory. Imagine the insidious poison he must have spewed at other, less academically inclined students.

My experiences with authority figures didn't get much better as I progressed through school. A guidance counselor, with a dismissive and bitter presence, declared, "you're not what they make you out to be," and then proceeded to withhold my test scores, effectively sabotaging my opportunity for dual enrollment. This same counselor, in a moment of breathtaking cruelty, told a teenage mother that she had "already ruined her life," and that she "wasn't going to be anything more than that." These were not isolated incidents of incompetence; they were systemic failures, deliberate acts of sabotage and cruelty disguised as guidance. These experiences taught me a harsh lesson: the systems designed to support and uplift young people can be deeply flawed, and the individuals entrusted with our well-being can be the very ones who inflict the most profound damage. I learned early on to approach authority and guidance with a healthy dose of skepticism, to question their motives, and to trust my own instincts, for clearly, those meant to serve as guides could be the architects of our destruction.

Yet another instance of systemic failure that continues to haunt me is a bus accident in middle school. It remains etched in my memory, a scene playing out in sharp detail, despite the passage of time. It was a pre-dawn morning, the darkness still clinging to the world. I was standing on the bus, styling a friend's hair for "hobo day," when the wheels lurched, detached from the road, once, then again. My small frame bounced with each impact, and I instinctively assumed we had hit a deer, a common occurrence in our rural landscape. But it wasn't a deer. It was a child, waiting at his bus stop, a child on his way to the elementary school down the street. We remained on the bus as the near-lifeless body was airlifted, only to learn later that he had died. We were then transported to school, confined to the cafeteria for hours, before being dismissed to class, without a single word of guidance or support. The silence was deafening. Whispers about the bus driver circulated, blame was informally assigned, but no one, no administrator, offered us an opportunity to process the trauma we had just experienced. I don't think I ever truly processed it…until now.

Before moving on, I must acknowledge the pervasive fear and confusion that permeated my middle school years, the constant anxiety of potential assault. In that environment, such violations had become normalized, a grim reality of daily life. I remember the bathroom, the supposed sanctuary, becoming a site of violation, groups of pre-teen fingers penetrating my young body. My reactions were a mix of fear and confusion, my sexual immaturity amplifying the sense of helplessness and conflicting arousal. The teachers seemed oblivious, or perhaps willfully ignorant, of the chaos unfolding. I learned to unlock classroom windows, to escape through them, to avoid the hallway, to avoid becoming the next victim. It was a calculated risk, a desperate attempt to maintain control in a world that felt utterly out of control.

I remember the irony of being enrolled in the 'Gifted Education' program at the same middle school, a designation that, in our resource-scarce environment, seemed more a label than a reality. With so few students qualifying, the promised enrichment never materialized. Instead, I found myself relegated to a regular Exceptional Student Education (ESE) class, a space where my academic role was less about advancement and more about remediation. My task was to tutor students struggling with fundamental skills, like basic reading comprehension. Here I was, legally entitled to a more challenging and stimulating academic experience, yet I was effectively repurposed as a teacher's aide, sacrificing my own intellectual growth to support others. The frustration was palpable, a constant dissonance between my potential and the reality of my daily routine. I felt trapped, my own educational needs sidelined, my potential stifled. The system, designed to nurture and cultivate talent, had instead become a barrier, a testament to its own inherent flaws. Ultimately, I made the difficult decision to opt out of the 'Gifted' program altogether. It was a tacit admission of defeat, a surrender to the limitations of a system that had failed to recognize and nurture my potential. It was a choice born of disillusionment, a stark realization that my own educational journey would have to be forged outside the confines of a system that had clearly abandoned me.

Now, let me shift to a slightly lighter tone, though the weight of these experiences remains. Despite the trauma, I am grateful for my rural upbringing. It shaped me, it challenged me, and it instilled within me a desire to disrupt the limitations of that environment, to expand horizons, to bring exposure and understanding to a world often confined by its own boundaries.

The limitations of knowledge, the systemic failures, extended beyond the realm of trauma. Financial literacy was a foreign concept, and the resources for guidance were scarce. When I went to college, I accepted every student loan offered, not out of necessity, but out of fear. I worked hard, earned scholarships, and supplemented my income, but I felt a deep-seated insecurity, a fear that I would be left without recourse if something unexpected happened. The systemic disappointment of a $250 credit card limit, and the lack of a safety net, led me to accumulate a mountain of debt. The reality of the outstanding balance upon graduation was a stark awakening. I was expecting my first child, needed time to adjust to motherhood, and later pursued graduate degrees, further adding to the financial burden. I became a "legal hustler," teaching at multiple institutions to make ends meet. It was a system I created out of ignorance and survival, a system that, while functional, carried long-term consequences. I wish I had known better.

The failures extended to the family structure. My parents' divorce, though seemingly amicable, was a rupture that left lasting scars. I remember the vain attempts to reunite them, the tears shed as I carried my father's belongings back into the house. The shock of discovering his new family, the betrayal I felt, the realization that I had been clinging to a false hope. The system of family, had failed me. Adding to the complexity, my parents had fostered a child with severe disabilities just before the divorce. When the system learned of the separation, they removed the child, deeming the home unstable. However, the relative who took custody quickly realized they couldn't handle his needs and my mother, despite the circumstances, took him back with open, albeit unsupported, arms. That child, once a vulnerable infant, is now a man approaching forty, a testament to my mother's unconditional commitment.

Passion Calls

The pervasive "you don't know what you don't know" mentality, which I initially attributed to financial woes, permeated every aspect of my life. The school system, the community, they all played a role in limiting my exposure to the world beyond the rural landscape. Extracurricular activities were scarce, field trips were rare, and career discussions were confined to a narrow range of options – corrections, state jobs, nursing, teaching, law, military, medicine. Anything beyond that was left to chance, to self-discovery. When I arrived at the university, my desire to write was met with suggestions to pursue law, a more "practical" path. I yearned to write, to weave words into worlds, to capture the essence of people and emotions. But the siren call of security, the primal need to provide for myself and a future family, drowned out the whispers of my creative soul. Eventually, I was steered towards the pragmatic realms of engineering and ultimately, industrial engineering. These were not inherently bad choices, but they were choices born of perceived necessity, of a calculated risk aversion, not the unfettered exploration of my passions. The pragmatic voice offered stability, of tangible outcomes, of a path paved with predictable success.

The creative voice, however, was relegated to the margins, a silent yearning, a dream deferred. And so, I found myself, always the writer among my engineering colleagues, channeling my creative energy into technical jargon, into the precise language of algorithms and systems. The poetry of my soul was translated into the logic of code and the efficiency of processes. But the longing remained, a persistent undercurrent, a quiet rebellion against the constraints of practicality.

Finally, after the arduous journey of earning three degrees in engineering and a master's degree in business, I stand at a threshold. The chains of perceived necessity have loosened, the whispers of my creative spirit have grown louder, and I am finally free to write. To write not just technical reports, but to write the stories that have been simmering within me, to give voice to the experiences that have shaped me, to embrace my true love, the art of storytelling. It is a homecoming, a return to the essence of who I am, a liberation from the confines of a path chosen out of fear, and not much more than a chain of failed systems.

Resilience Rising

From a shattered home, a fragile start,

A childhood marked by wounded heart.

Amidst the chaos, a spirit gleams,

A covenant of hope, defying dreams.

Through trauma's storm, she navigated the way,

A resilience born, day-by-day.

With limited means, she dared to soar,

A warrior's spirit, forevermore.

Though darkness lingered, hope would shine,

A future bright, a path divine.

With scars that healed, a strength she'd find,

A testament to a resilient mind.

Day 5

The Digital Mirror

The digital mirror is a reflection not of flesh and bone, but of pixels and curated realities. A world where validation is quantified in likes, and self-worth is measured in followers. I remember a time, a simpler time, when I moved through the world with an unburdened spirit, oblivious to the scrutinizing gaze of others. I fashioned my own style, a rebellious blend of bargain finds and self-made creations, topped with a daring half-wig, a statement of unapologetic individuality. I added a touch of sparkle, a bit of height, ensuring my presence was felt. But the external response, the judgment of "them," never truly penetrated my armor. Once I stepped into a room, I erected an invisible barrier, a fortress of self-assurance, convinced that I was everything I needed to be. This feeling, this heightened sense of self, was a constant companion, a shield against the world's opinions.

But the world changed. The age of information and access ushered in the era of social media, a digital landscape that has become an inextricable part of our daily lives. These platforms, virtual communities connecting people across geographical and cultural boundaries, offer undeniable benefits. Global connections, instant communication, access to information – the possibilities are vast. Yet, beneath the surface of connectivity lies a darker current, a profound impact on our culture, our self-confidence, and our very sense of belonging. And I, like so many others, have felt the insidious creep of this digital influence.

At first, I tried to distance myself, to minimize my engagement with the relentless scroll and the curated realities. But in doing so, I've found myself navigating a strange paradox. While I crave the space and mental clarity that comes with digital detachment, I also experience a growing sense of isolation. Almost everyone I know exists within these platforms. My professional networks rely on them for communication and collaboration.

Entire industries and digital economies have sprung up, fueled by social media's reach and influence. It feels as though I'm faced with an impossible choice: embrace the pros and cons, navigate the toxic currents, and remain connected, or opt out entirely, joining the dwindling ranks of the digitally detached, and risk being left behind, an outsider looking in at a world that continues to evolve at breakneck speed.

Allow me to provide a stark illustration of this insidious shift. When I first ventured into the realm of social media, I approached it with a sense of detachment, a naive belief that I could control its influence. I'd post a picture, a thought, a fleeting moment, and then walk away, never looking back. I'd said what I needed to say, released it into the digital ether, and felt a sense of closure, a freedom to move on. There was a purity to that detachment, a sense of autonomy.

Gradually, however, the allure of engagement began to creep in. I started returning to my posts, initially out of curiosity, then out of a growing desire to see the responses, to gauge the reactions. I'd scroll through the comments, a mix of validation and critique, feeling a fleeting sense of connection, a momentary boost to my ego. And then, the inevitable slide.

Recently, I found myself compulsively returning to my posts, feeling the need to respond to comments, seeking the fleeting dopamine hit of digital interaction. I had become a participant in the very system I had initially sought to avoid, a slave to the algorithm, a performer in the digital theater of self-presentation.

Who is that girl, that desperate seeker of validation? The reflection in the digital mirror was becoming increasingly unrecognizable, a distorted image of the confident, self-assured woman I once believed myself to be. The realization was a jolt, a cold splash of water, a stark reminder of how easily we can lose ourselves in the pursuit of digital approval.

Perhaps the most pervasive impact of social media is the erosion of our individual sense of self. The constant barrage of carefully curated images, the idealized portrayals of lives lived to the fullest, creates a relentless cycle of comparison. We measure our own realities against these digital fictions, these highlight reels of perfection, and inevitably, we fall short.

The relentless pursuit of likes and followers, the craving for external validation, distorts our sense of self-worth, leaving us feeling inadequate, anxious, and perpetually lacking. This phenomenon, the insidious creep of "social media anxiety," has become a pervasive mental health crisis, a silent epidemic fueled by the relentless pursuit of digital approval.

The growing need for validation through likes and comments is inextricably linked to the dangerous practice of idolization. We project our own desires, our own insecurities, onto the carefully crafted personas we encounter online. We believe that by emulating their success, their appearance, their lifestyle, we will somehow attain the happiness and fulfillment that eludes us. But this idolization is a mirage, a dangerous illusion that leads us down a path of inauthenticity. We sacrifice our individuality, our unique perspectives, our genuine selves, in an attempt to conform to unrealistic standards, to chase the approval of a digital audience.

To break free from this cycle, to reclaim my authentic self, I've learned the importance of cultivating a healthy relationship with these platforms. This involves setting boundaries, limiting my time online, and consciously challenging the narratives I encounter. It means recognizing the inherent artificiality of social media, the carefully constructed personas, the edited realities. It means remembering that behind every flawless image, every witty caption, every seemingly perfect life, there is a human being, with flaws, insecurities, and struggles just like my own.

More importantly, it means cultivating a strong sense of self-worth that is rooted in my own values, my own experiences, my own internal compass, not in the approval of a digital audience. It's about developing a deeper understanding of my own strengths, my own passions, my own unique contributions to the world. It's about recognizing that my worth is not determined by the number of likes I receive, but by the integrity of my actions, the compassion of my heart, and the authenticity of my spirit. By embracing my true self, by celebrating my individuality, I can resist the pressure to conform, to idolize, to lose myself in the digital mirror. I can reclaim my power, my voice, my authentic being.

Digital Mirror's Gaze

Caught in the digital mirror's gaze...

A world of pixels, a curated stage,

Where likes and follows assign value to a page.

A woman's anxious voice, a vulnerable plea to engage,

Seeking validation from a stranger, her relevance gauged.

Caught in the digital mirror's gaze...

Idolizing illusions, albeit a distorted view,

Chasing likes and attention, from an inevitable skew.

Authenticity fades, losing sight of virtue,

Trapped in a mirror maze, humility and values subdued.

Caught in the digital mirror's gaze...

Daring to break free, to a more conscious mind,

A quest to embrace flaws and truly present times.

Beyond the digital mirror, her true self defined,

Confident and authentic, uniquely designed.

Ultimately, rejecting the digital mirror's bind.

Day 6

Intersections of Identity

A theoretical framework that once held a certain intellectual allure, now a lived reality, an instinctive understanding of the interplay among social and political identities. I remember immersing myself in the concept of intersectionality, meticulously dissecting how race, gender, class, religion, and other factors intertwined to create unique experiences of oppression and privilege. It was more of an academic exercise, a way to understand the complexities of the world around me. But then, life intervened, shattering the theoretical constructs and forcing me to confront the lived reality of these intersections.

I spent countless hours trying to compartmentalize, to balance each identity, to create a harmonious equilibrium. But the task proved far more complex, a somewhat vain attempt to impose order on the chaos of my experience. Identities, I discovered, are not static; they are fluid, transient, constantly shifting in response to life's unpredictable currents. And when these currents become turbulent, when significant life events disrupt the delicate balance of our intersecting identities, we are left adrift, facing a profound identity crisis. This is where I find myself.

My personal journey over the last few years has been a series of seismic shifts, a cascade of disruptions that have shaken the very foundation of my being. The abandonment by my husband, a betrayal that shattered my sense of security and belonging. The loss of my father, my spiritual leader, a void that echoed with the absence of guidance and unconditional love. The isolating grip of the pandemic, a forced retreat from the world, a stark confrontation with my own solitude. To have my time with my children, my constant source of joy, divided, descended as a powerful and crippling blow. The devastating loss of my best friends, in a moment no one saw coming. The abrupt termination of my career as a systems engineering professor, a blow to my professional identity, a loss of purpose and direction. And the accumulation of poor financial decisions, a consequence of chaos and uncertainty, a manifestation of my inability to navigate the storm. These events, these intersections of loss and disruption, have left me adrift, disoriented, lost in an entanglement of intersecting spaces.

The spaces that once defined my existence – work, home, family, community – have become alien landscapes, devoid of familiarity. Looking in the mirror, once a simple act of self-recognition, has become a disorienting experience. I am confronted with a stranger, a reflection of someone I no longer recognize. Or perhaps, I see nothing at all, a blank canvas where the roles that once defined me – wife, daughter, professor – have been erased, leaving behind an empty space, a void that feels impossible to fill.

The concept of free agency, once a symbol of liberation, has become a double-edged sword. The absence of constraints, the freedom from the expectations of previous identities, offers a sense of boundless possibility. But without the familiar anchors of work, family, and community, I am wandering in a vast, featureless desert, the sun beating down, no landmarks to guide me, struggling to find sustenance and direction in the barren expanse. The freedom to choose, to define my own path, has become a burden, a paralyzing weight of uncertainty.

The intersectionality of spaces, once a source of support and belonging, has become a suffocating web of isolation. When these spaces are in harmony, when they reinforce each other, they provide a sense of purpose, a feeling of being grounded. But when they are disrupted, when they collide and contradict, they create a disorienting sense of loss, a feeling of being untethered, disconnected from the world and from myself.

Navigating this maze requires more than just external exploration; it demands a deep dive into the recesses of my own being. It is a journey of self-discovery, a quest to reclaim my identity, to redefine myself in the face of adversity. It is a process of dismantling the old narratives, of shedding the layers of expectation and illusion, and of embracing the raw, authentic truth of my existence. It is a journey that is as much internal as it is external, a quest to rediscover my identity. It is a process of rebuilding, of weaving together the fragments of my shattered self, of creating a new narrative, a new understanding of who I am and who I am meant to be. It is a journey of reclaiming my voice, my power, my authentic self. It is a journey of shifting.

Spaces

A convolution of spaces, once abundantly clear,

Now hid amongst mist, filled with uncertainty and fear.

Intersections of roles, such a fragile art,

Shattered by loss, betrayal, and still, torn apart.

The mirror selfishly reflects a stranger's face.

"Who is she?" "What happened to her",

An absence of guiding grace.

Free agency, a blunt and still, double-edged blade.

Once a liberation, an opportunity, a path unafraid.

Yet in this massive void of identities lost, a little spark remains.

A tiny mustard seed of faith, that yields the power to sustain.

Through the shattered fragments, a renewed self to find.

Choosing a raw journey inward, toward a peace of mind.

Day 7

Belonging Nowhere

Belonging. It's a concept I've wrestled with, a phantom limb that aches with its absence. Just like the intricate systems I analyze as an engineer, the systems of social connection, of community, of self, have consistently revealed their flaws in my life. Today, then, is a dissection of these fractured spaces, the places where I've found myself an outsider, a misplaced cog in the machine.

It started subtly, a slow drift away from the familiar. Growing up in my rural hometown, the bonds were tight, the rhythms predictable. But as I ventured out, as I absorbed new knowledge and experiences, the old connections began to fray. I'd try to exchange insights, to bridge the gap, but the conversations would fall flat, the shared interests dissolving into a chasm of disinterest. It wasn't malice, just a widening of perspectives, a realization that we were diverging onto different paths. The system of shared experience, once a sturdy foundation, was crumbling.

Then came the professional realm, the world of academia. As a Black woman, a systems engineering professor, I was a novelty, a statistic to be trotted out when diversity was the topic du jour. I was the token, the representative, always volunteered for DEI initiatives, always acutely aware of the stark contrast between myself and my colleagues. The labs, the faculty meetings, the conferences – spaces dominated by faces that bore no resemblance to mine, backgrounds that were worlds apart. I remember that first work trip, the humiliation of standing at the hotel desk, my PhD a useless piece of paper against the reality of an empty bank account. I had a whole lot of student loans, a newborn and toddler, and a brand-new PhD but not enough money for incidentals at the hotel my employer had prepaid for.

And then, the incident at the pre-conference reception, a gathering of Chief Operating Officers (COO) from Fortune 500 companies. The evening was a suite of pale professionals, a sea of tailored suits. I, in my most vibrant,

Federica-esque attire – a bold, intricately cut wide leg pant suit that reflected my high spirits – was engaged in conversation with the Dean's secretary, the only other woman present, albeit a white woman. Suddenly, a white man, a COO, strode across the room, interrupting our exchange with an unexpected request. "Can you go get me some hot sauce," he commanded of me, his tone laced with an assumption that cut through the veneer of sophistication. My carefully constructed facade, the image of a poised, accomplished professor, shattered in an instant. There were no servers in the room; it was a mingling event. Yet, this man, without hesitation, designated me as the help. The request wasn't just absurd; it was a calculated jab, a blatant display of implicit bias. It wasn't about the hot sauce; it was about the insidious undercurrent of being perpetually "othered," reduced to a stereotype, stripped of my professional identity I'd worked so hard to achieve. It was a stark reminder that even in a room of supposed equals, the deeply ingrained systems of perceived social hierarchy remained stubbornly intact, casting me as an outsider, a servant, in a space where I was meant to be a peer.

The sense of displacement extended beyond the professional realm. Even in my own home, in the affluent, predominantly white enclave of a South Florida golf course, I felt like an anomaly. The manicured lawns and pristine facades masked a subtle but pervasive sense of exclusion. The system of social belonging, defined by shared demographics and cultural norms, was one I could never fully infiltrate.

And then, the internal conflict, the sense of not belonging even in my own skin. The cultural pressure to conform, to adhere to a narrow definition of beauty and success, to being black, to being a woman, to constantly prove my worth – it is a weight that never lifted. The system of societal expectations, particularly for Black women, is a relentless force, demanding constant vigilance and self-regulation. How should I speak? Who am I allowed to speak to? Did I use the right tone? Should I suppress my accent? Do they hear me? Is the understanding mutual?

Even interactions with the medical system revealed the same insidious pattern, a stark illustration of how systemic bias can infiltrate even the most supposedly objective spaces. I recall sitting in a dermatologist's office, a doctorate holder myself, driving a newer Suburban, dressed in what I considered ordinary, professional attire. I was there to address a specific skin condition, seeking treatment options. Instead, the doctor's response was a condescending dismissal. "That treatment," she said, her tone laced with implication, "is very expensive and, frankly, not really designed for Black skin. You should just try a wipe." A wipe? For a condition requiring a specialist? I was led to press her for the actual cost, which, to my disbelief, was a mere $300 – a sum she had implied was prohibitive. Then, as if to further underscore her assumptions, she requested a $30 co-pay, asking, with a thinly veiled skepticism, "Is that going to be too much for you to pay today?" I was dumbfounded. What about my presence, my education, my PPO insurance, suggested I couldn't afford a simple co-pay? It was a blatant display of prejudice, a reminder that even in a professional setting, even as a paying patient seeking care, I was still subject to the insidious scrutiny of societal biases.

The dismissive doctor, the condescending assumptions, the blatant disregard for my concerns – it was a microcosm of the larger societal biases that permeated every aspect of my life. The system of healthcare, designed to serve all, was failing me, failing us.

The examples are endless, a relentless stream of moments that reinforced the same unsettling truth: I didn't belong.

Somewhere along the way came a stark, unsettling realization: to the world's eye, I am Black first. Not professor, not mother, not engineer, not female, but Black. It's a lens through which every achievement, every interaction, every facet of my being is filtered. This awareness was a harsh awakening, a constant undertone ripe with limitations, of preconceived notions, of a battle fought on a playing field already tilted. Perhaps this is why I instinctively tried to distance myself from the very stereotypes that, in truth, were a part of my heritage. I sought refuge in spaces where I wasn't defined by my skin, where I could simply be 'me,' even if that meant denying a part of myself. I often ran from 'Black' groups, from experiences that might 'isolate' me from the wider world, believing assimilation was the key to acceptance. But I am Black, undeniably, and beautifully so. And the yearning for community within my own community, the desire to feel a sense of belonging among those who truly understand my experience, is just as vital as any sense of acceptance I sought to build in the broader world. It's a recognition that wholeness comes not from denying a part of myself, but embracing the entirety of who I am.

In my experience, the systems of community, of profession, of even my own identity, are fractured, flawed, and ultimately, exclusionary. And as I navigate these unsettled spaces, I'm left with questions: Is what I seek in "belonging" a place, a feeling, or a state of being? What does true belonging even look like in a world so fractured? How do I build a sense of belonging when the very systems designed to provide it are rigged against me, and people like me? And how do we dismantle the exclusionary structures without replicating the very patterns we seek to destroy?

Unsettled Noise

In rooms of power, a phantom guest,

Qualified, still marginalized, with no room for rest.

A looming shadow cast, in borrowed light,

A fractured mirror, accompanies the muddled sense of sight.

Between multiple worlds, such a lonely stride,

Where roots are lost, and conflicting truths collide.

The skin a hyper visible mark, her voice a loud yet muted plea,

A constant battle raging, both external and internally.

No safe retreat, no place where she can hide,

Just haunting echoes, where unpleasant memories deride.

A fervent wish, for a genuine and unconditional embrace,

To cut through the noise victoriously, to their dismay.

Day 8

The Fabric of Facades

I've been pondering something, a thought that haunts my days, a peculiar fixation, if you will. It's my act of transformation, of slipping into another skin, another persona. I've done this my entire life. I'd never thought about the implications of my hobbies, but I will say that I have an affinity for dressing up and dressing down. I love characters, real or of my own imagination. Is there a reason I enjoy the transformation so much? Am I more comfortable outside of my own skin? Or am I overthinking the connections. At this point I really don't know. Characters…dressing up, costumes, role play…hmm…

It's another system, isn't it? The system of identity, or perhaps, the lack thereof. Just like the systems of my childhood, the ones that failed so spectacularly, this urge to alter my appearance, to become someone else, it feels like a response. A reaction. A symptom, even.

Today, then, unwraps this compulsion, this need to transform. It's a bit like taking apart a complex machine, trying to understand why a gear turns a certain way, why a lever pulls in a particular direction. I'm attempting to disassemble the layers of myself, the ones I've carefully constructed, and those that have been thrust upon me.

I remember, as a child, creating elaborate costumes from scraps of fabric and discarded items. I was never just playing; I was becoming. A pirate, a queen, a space explorer, a disco dancer, anyone but myself. I didn't realize it then but it was a form of escape, a way to navigate a world that often felt overwhelming and unsafe. Just like the stories of trauma, the failed systems of my youth, these costumes were a way to control my narrative, to dictate my reality.

Perhaps it's a coping mechanism, a way to deal with the inherent instability I felt growing up. If the world around me was unpredictable, if the adults in my life were unreliable, then I could at least control who I was in my own little world. I could become someone strong, someone powerful, someone invulnerable, someone who commanded attention.

But as I grew older, the costumes became more sophisticated, more nuanced. They weren't just physical transformations; they were emotional ones as well. I learned to play different roles, to adapt to different situations, to become whatever was needed of me. The good student, the helpful friend, the strong woman. These were all characters I played, each with their own set of rules, allure, and expectations.

And just like those childhood costumes, these roles were a way to protect myself. A way to avoid vulnerability, to keep people at a distance. I'd seen what happened when you let your guard down, when you trusted too easily. I'd seen the pain and the betrayal, the consequences of failed systems. So, I built my own system of facades, a network of masks that allowed me to navigate the world without ever truly being seen.

It's a strange paradox, isn't it? The desire to be seen, to be understood, while simultaneously hiding behind a carefully crafted persona. It's like trying to build a house of cards in a hurricane, constantly shifting and adjusting to avoid collapse.

But what happens when the hurricane subsides? What happens when the masks start to slip, when the roles become too heavy to bear? That's where I find myself now, in the aftermath of a storm, trying to piece together the fragments of my identity.

I'm realizing that these costumes, these roles, they're not just a way to escape; they're also a way to avoid confronting my own pain, my own fears. They're a distraction, a way to keep myself busy so I don't have to face the uncomfortable truths about who I am and what I've been through.

And that's the real challenge, isn't it? To strip away the layers, to shed the costumes, and to stand naked and vulnerable before the world. To embrace the messiness, the imperfections, the raw and unfiltered truth of my own existence.

It's a terrifying prospect, but it's also liberating. To finally stop pretending, to finally be myself, whatever that means. To dismantle the systems of self-deception and embrace the possibility of a truly authentic life.

Like a system engineer pulling apart a complex machine, I am taking apart the systems of my own being. I'm looking for the broken parts, the faulty wiring, the misaligned gears. And I'm determined to rebuild myself, not as a collection of roles and masks, but as a whole, integrated, and unapologetic me.

Beneath the Masks

Beneath the laced veil reside a carefully hidden face.

A many roles- shifting, awaiting- its time and place.

Each costume worn, a fun yet fragile shield,

From truths unseen, and varied wounds unhealed.

The stage is set, the lights grow dim,

It's showtime!

For your entertainment!

Let the show begin!

To shed the guise, the point where the performance must end,

A naked soul remains, and an inner peace transcends.

Resilience blooms fiercely, strengths asserted untamed,

Authenticity and integrity!

Purpose and meaning!

And growth, she ultimately claimed.

Day 9

And the Wheels Fell Off

One day the carefully constructed web of facades crumbled, and on that day the wheels, quite literally, fell off. It wasn't a gradual descent; it was a precipitous drop, a sudden and brutal unraveling. The catalyst, as for so many, was COVID-19. But the cracks in the system, the underlying vulnerabilities, had been there all along.

The world shrank, confined to the four walls of our home. My children, once vibrant and engaged in the world, were now tethered to screens, their education reduced to a chaotic stream of virtual lessons. Managing four children – a newborn, a toddler slated for daycare, an elementary schooler, and a middle schooler – navigating the inconsistent online teaching of overwhelmed educators, it was an impossible task. So, "Boom Bang Living and Learning" was born, a defiant act of control in a world spinning out of control. I became their homeschool teacher, their sole source of education, nearly their catchall.

My husband, however, claimed he needed "more time" to transition his job. Months blurred into a stark reality: I was a single parent, legally married but utterly alone, in a strange town, homeschooling four children and managing a new house. The systems I'd relied upon – shared responsibilities, a supportive network – vanished, leaving me truly alone for the first time. Yet, even this wasn't the full extent of the unraveling. I remember calling a hotel about a lost watch, only to be met with confusion because my account showed numerous stays – though I'd only been there once. Another piece of stability crumbled. Then, a Zelle notification from our joint account for "half our hotel stay" from a woman who later declared her love for my husband. These insights were not things I sought; they were revelations forced upon me, each a shattering blow, another wheel falling off.

My journey hasn't been a sequence of isolated incidents; it's been a relentless, escalating cascade of seismic shifts, and apparently, I'm navigating life with the resilience of a semi-truck, even as its wheels continue to detach. The year prior, my father, a pastor, my confidante, my anchor, had been ripped from my life. Guilt, a relentless tormentor, gnawed at me with the "what ifs" that echoed endlessly in my mind. I was haunted by the memory of his holiday visit, my failure to notice he'd forgotten his medication. When his blood sugar spiked to an unreadable level, I rushed him to the VA hospital, only to be met with a dismissive nurse, his judgment clouded by prejudice or perhaps exhaustion as it was during a government shutdown. He saw a large, disoriented Black man and assumed intoxication, dismissing my desperate pleas that he was a diabetic with heart disease. My dad didn't drink! The saline solution, a fatal misstep for a heart patient in diabetic shock, the rushed, inadequate care – it was a system betraying him, betraying me. My voice, as always, was drowned. My father, dead from a catastrophic cascade of medical errors: a stroke, a diabetic coma, and last, a heart attack.

It was Friday, January 4th, in the humid air of South Florida. I was a prisoner of my own guilt, grappling with the logistical nightmare of transporting my 56-year-old father's body back to North Florida, piecing together funds and support for a dignified burial, leading my family, navigating the complexities of his recent divorce, and all while carrying my fourth child, three months into a pregnancy. Monday, January 6th, loomed, and with it, the start of a new semester, a full teaching load at my university. I reached out to my leadership, pleading for a reprieve, a moment to breathe, to grieve. They responded with cold bureaucracy, informing me that the university lacked any mechanism to accommodate my situation. I was expected to teach. But how? My grief was a physical weight, crushing me. I tried, I desperately tried, but my performance, my enthusiasm, my very desire to function, plummeted. I was a shell, hollowed out by loss, and the system, once again, offered no solace.

The pattern of professional betrayal that had begun before my father's passing, continued unabated. With the change of my direct supervisor, a once-respected faculty member transformed into a conduit for personal attacks. My new boss consistently belittled me and my work, often revealing he hadn't even bothered to examine it. He deliberately sabotaged my reputation across the University, sometimes doing so in front of myself and witnesses. He systematically silenced me in meetings, skipping my turn after everyone else had spoken. He actively excluded me from departmental projects, even when I was the more qualified, opting for external consultants or new hires instead. He obstructed approvals for service work and expenditures, a clear attempt to limit my professional growth. I lodged informal complaints, detailing this calculated assault on my confidence and worth. His supervisor's response was a chilling admission: "We know he's a poor leader, not suited for the role. Just be patient while we address this." His boss started to approve a subset of my requests directly, until I eventually stopped asking. Years passed, and the institution's response? A promotion for my predator. A non-supervisory role at the College level.

And the organizational system continued to disappoint.

When COVID hit, my university expected "business as usual." There was no consideration for the fact that my children were now home around the clock, that I was juggling multiple roles, that the very essence of my life had been torn apart. The relentless pressure, the constant stress, the grief that I'd never addressed, it took its toll. Car accidents, a fall down the stairs, the physical and emotional trauma compounded. A head injury, chronic back pain, crippling anxiety, and a profound sense of isolation just became too much. My body, my mind, my spirit – they were breaking.

I did take a short-term disability leave, but a cruel twist of fate interfered. A lawsuit, which had been covering the physician who initially placed me on leave, reached a settlement. This abruptly terminated my care, as they only treated patients with an active lawsuit. To continue my disability, I needed their signature, an "impossibility". I was navigating the unfamiliar disability process with little understanding given my injuries and mental state, already struggling with the financial strain of reduced pay. Desperate, I opted for what seemed like the easiest route: returning to work. I asked my chiropractor, the medical professional that was readily accessible, to provide a note outlining the accommodations he could vouch for, knowing full well I was in no condition to perform my job. Unsurprisingly, no accommodations were granted.

Again, I tried. I truly tried. Some days, my body was a prison, immobile. Some days, my mind was a blank slate, the alphabet a foreign language. Some days, my head was a chaotic fireworks display of pain. Some days, the tears wouldn't stop. Everyone knew I shouldn't have returned, but no one from my workplace offered the assistance I needed. It wasn't until I was asked to resign, mere moments before the start of a new semester, and called into the office to "wet sign" my release papers, that they suddenly feigned concern. "You should really have an advocate!" they said. "Do you want us to call EAP with you?" "I can't let you leave without a mental health check-in at the hospital." The hypocrisy was staggering. How dare the system display such concern and capability *after* the damage was done? I had just signed away the career I'd built over fifteen years, a mere five minutes prior. It was shocking but even more appalling.

The loss was just another addition to my devastation. I lost my career, the professional identity I had painstakingly constructed. With it went the benefits I had counted on for my children – college tuition, health insurance, life insurance. I managed to maintain some service work within my technical community, but it is a struggle, as it is volunteer-based and self-funded. I had already lost my father, my unwavering source of support and guidance. I had lost my husband, the partner I had envisioned sharing my life with. And I'd lost moments of time with the children I'd always shared every notable moment with. And now, in the midst of this catastrophic unraveling, I lost myself. The question that had haunted me for so long – how do I reconcile the intersection of my identities? – was eclipsed by a more fundamental, more terrifying one: Who am I? The systems had failed, not just externally, but internally. The carefully constructed sense of self, the illusion of control, it had all shattered, leaving behind a void, an emptiness that stretched into the unknown. The plateau had been reached, not as a place of triumph, but as a desolate landscape of loss and uncertainty.

Spinning Wheels

A steady path, a sudden break,

The wheels unbound; the world suddenly shakes.

A jarring halt, an inconceivable sight,

Where shattered fragments, steal the light.

The ground gives way, beneath her feet,

A dizzying fall, a bitter defeat.

The spinning world, a blurred design,

Where the shattered pieces, fail to align.

The wheels fall off, a crashing blow,

No clear path forward, no help in tow.

Day 10

An Intoxicating Void

I have discovered the potent, almost addictive, power of loneliness.

At nearly forty years old, a stark and unsettling truth dawned upon me: I had never truly been alone. Not in the profound, existential sense. My life had been a constant hum of connection, roommates, family, career, and community. There were always roles to play, responsibilities to shoulder, people to care for. Even in moments of solitude, there was the comforting knowledge of a network, a safety net. But now, the net had vanished, leaving me suspended in a vast, empty space. Suddenly, there were stretches of time, long, echoing silences, when it was just me. No children clamoring for attention, no partner to share the day's events with, no professional obligations to distract me. Just the stark, unadorned reality of my own presence. It was a foreign landscape, a territory I had never explored, and the sheer unfamiliarity of it was both terrifying and strangely liberating. The absence of external noise amplified the internal chaos, forcing me to confront the questions I had long avoided. This wasn't just physical aloneness; it was a profound isolation, a stripping away of the external layers that had defined me, leaving me face-to-face with the raw, unfiltered essence of myself. And in that confrontation, I began to understand the true weight, and the unsettling power, of being utterly alone.

Loneliness, I've learned, is a master manipulator, an architect of desperation, and a catalyst for actions I never thought myself capable of.

I was adrift, untethered from the identities that had defined me. The professor, the wife, the daughter, the community pillar – all of them had dissolved, leaving behind an empty shell. I had never allowed myself the luxury of grief, of truly feeling the weight of my losses. I had always been the strong one, the problem solver, the one who kept moving forward. But now, there was no forward. There was only the suffocating silence, the relentless ache of absence.

The grief, it was a physical manifestation, a gnawing emptiness that mirrored the emotional void. I was forced to stop. To stop and feel the pain that had been building for years. To stop and acknowledge the losses, the failures, the betrayals. To stop and pray, to find some semblance of comfort in a universe that felt indifferent.

My first instinct, a testament to the desperation that loneliness breeds, was to seek a quick fix. I reached out to a television show, a reality program promising to "fix your life." I won't name the show, but suffice it to say, I was looking for an external force to magically erase the pain, to restore the order that had been so violently disrupted. I imagined a team of experts swooping in, transforming my chaos into a neatly packaged narrative of triumph. But the universe, in its infinite wisdom, or perhaps its cruel irony, denied me that escape. No one wanted to join me on the show. I was left alone, once again, to face the wreckage of my life.

Time passed, but the problems didn't. The physical pain, a constant reminder of the trauma my body had endured, became unbearable. The mental stack, once a carefully organized tower of strength, seemed to crumble with every passing day. I was trapped in a cycle of grief, unable to let go of the life that was, the life that should have been. The absence of family moments, the forced sharing of my children, the gaping holes where connection and support once resided – these voids became all-consuming.

And in my loneliness, I began to fill those voids, consciously and unconsciously, with whatever I could find. I found myself reaching for fleeting moments of connection, for temporary distractions, for anything that could dull the sharp edges of my pain. I was searching for a replacement for the lost pieces of my life, a way to recreate the sense of belonging that had been so violently ripped away. The intoxicating void of loneliness had me reaching for anything tangible. And in many cases, this seeking left me more fragile than I began.

The desperation to fill the emptiness manifested in a series of impulsive choices, a frantic attempt to patch the holes in my shattered existence. I clung to fleeting connections, mistaking temporary distractions for genuine intimacy. I sought validation in external sources, seeking affirmation in the eyes of strangers, in the fleeting approval of those who knew nothing of my true self. The desire to escape the suffocating silence drove me to seek out experiences that offered a momentary reprieve, a fleeting sense of purpose. But these temporary fixes, these superficial connections, only served to deepen the abyss of loneliness, leaving me feeling more isolated and vulnerable than before. Each failed attempt to recreate the lost sense of belonging chipped away at my already fragile sense of self, reinforcing the belief that I was irrevocably broken, and alone.

The search for a substitute for what was lost became a self-destructive cycle. I was like a drowning person grasping at straws, each failed attempt pulling me further under. I was vulnerable to manipulation, to exploitation, to any semblance of connection that promised to alleviate the pain. The lack of self-knowledge, the absence of a solid foundation, made me susceptible to the whims of others, to the allure of fleeting pleasures. The intoxicating void of loneliness, coupled with the desperate need to fill it, had created a perfect storm, leaving me up the creek without a paddle, vulnerable to any current that promised to carry me away. And more often than not, those currents led me further from myself, further from healing, and further into the depths of fragility.

The Loneliest Hour

<u>Sitting in her loneliest hour</u>

Such a barren landscape, etched in shades of gray,

Where noise join forces and obstacles tower,

Where loneliness reigns, and hopes decay.

<u>Somewhere along this loneliest hour</u>

Silent screams dissipate within the hollow space,

Colluding with tears wanting to assert their power,

Pouring uncontrollably, determined to leave their trace.

Festering in this loneliest hour

A gnawing ache accompanies a constant sting,

Searching unarmed, vulnerably among the unfamiliar dour

Yet solitude's chains, relentlessly cling.

Standing in this loneliest hour

No hands to hold, no voices but her own to hear,

Unable to appreciate the positives of bower

Consumed by the empty echoes abound, drawing ever near.

Proceeding in the loneliest hour

The void consumes, an intoxicating pain without reprieve

The heart increasingly numbed, the spirit turning sour.

As empty depths, blinded eyes and the ensuing storm succeed.

Day 11

The Company You Keep

The day I confronted the harsh reality of the company I kept, a lesson etched in the raw vulnerability of my darkest hours. It wasn't merely about the people I chose to surround myself with; it was about the insidious ways in which their presence, their energy, their very essence, could shape and distort my own. Loneliness, I discovered, wasn't just an internal void; it was a vacuum that drew in whatever was nearby, regardless of its worth. And in my state of mind, I had allowed the wrong people to fill that space.

I've always been a person who empowers, a believer in the inherent potential of others. I see the spark, the hidden talent, the dormant strength. I see the pain of the past, the failed systems and the eventual impact. But in my shattered state, this strength became a weakness, a self-destructive compulsion. I tried to breathe "ability" into those around me, to lift them from their stagnation, to ignite a fire within their souls. But I failed to recognize a fundamental truth: some people are content in their dormancy. Some people have no desire to change, to evolve, to rise. And in my attempts to elevate them, I only emptied myself, draining my own reserves of energy and hope.

I found myself entangled in dynamics with a person riddled with self-destructive habits. I became a self-appointed savior, a tireless advocate, attempting to break their patterns by exposing different ways of thinking and being. But in the process, I became a mirror, reflecting their flaws, adopting their negativity. I was morphing into the very essence of the person I was trying to help, a grotesque parody of my former self. My efforts were ineffective, a Sisyphean task, because they were content in their circumstance, comfortable in their stagnation. And in that comfort, I joined them

The illusion of authenticity, the image I had cultivated, the belief I held about myself, all ceased to exist after the wheels fell off. The people I encountered in my isolation, they saw the cracks, the vulnerabilities, the raw, exposed nerves. And they exploited them. They pierced my defenses, infiltrated my psyche, and affected me in ways I had never allowed before.

"I just finished my systems engineering children's books," I announced, my voice filled with a fragile hope.

"Nobody cares about systems," came the dismissive reply, a casual dismissal that sent a tremor of doubt through my core. I retreated, second-guessing my work.

"You only help me because you want to be with me," a voice accused, twisting my offered hand into a selfish act.

"Not at all," I replied, the words a shield against the cynicism. "I choose to help you because I am kind, I care, and I genuinely want the best for people." But the words, once a source of strength, now echoed with a hollow resonance, a testament to the erosion of my own belief in their truth.

"You're gaining weight," another voice remarked, a casual observation that became a cruel indictment.

"Ok, I will just get some work done to take care of that," I retorted, a desperate attempt to reclaim control that left me feeling inadequate.

"I need help," I pleaded, my voice trembling as I was learning how to ask for help.

"Oh, I'm not available," came the unconcerned reply, a cold reminder of isolation washing over me.

"But I've always helped you, have even offered before you asked because I witnessed your need," I stammered, disbelief creeping in.

"Sorry," they shrugged, "my other priorities come first."

What I found out about myself was that I didn't know how to say "no," how to set boundaries, how to protect my energy. I was a vessel, constantly depleted, constantly giving, constantly sacrificing myself for others. I was invisible, yielding to the whims and demands of those around me, allowing them to define my worth, to dictate my path.

I've learned through bitter trial - the impact of the people around you is not just a matter of influence; it's a matter of survival. They can be your anchors, grounding you in your truth, reminding you of your strength. Or they can be your weights, dragging you down into their own depths of negativity and self-destruction. In my vulnerability, I had chosen the weights, allowing them to pull me under, to drown me in their own despair.

But even in the depths of despair, there is hope. The realization, however painful, is a catalyst for change. The awareness of the toxic influence is the first step towards liberation. I began to understand that healing wasn't just about addressing my internal wounds, but also about creating a sanctuary, a space where I could nurture my spirit, surrounded by those who uplift and inspire me. I needed to learn to choose my company wisely, to surround myself with those who reflect the best version of myself, who believe in my potential, who see the spark within me and help me fan it into a flame. I needed to redirect my love towards those who could reciprocate it. It was a lesson learned in the crucible of loneliness, a lesson that has greatly informed my self-awareness, and shaped my journey towards healing.

A Tainted Circle

A fragile heart, in lonely plight,

Drew shadows in, to dim the light.

Empowerment's gift, turned poisoned dart,

As empty souls, tore her apart.

Please, child, turn back, it's all very cunning,

you're going the wrong way, honey!

A mirror held, reflecting pain,

Adopting flaws, in a toxic rain.

Dismissive words, a wounding sting,

Doubt's heavy chains, upon a broken wing.

They're leading you astray, the jokes aren't funny,

you're going the wrong way, honey!

No boundaries set, no strength to hold,

Invisible yields, a story unfolds.

The company kept, a stark reveal,

An even more fractured self, she seeks to heal.

Those roads lead to ruin, a dark and empty dunny,

you're going the wrong way, honey!

Day 12

A Frozen Frame

Dissociation. A word that once felt clinical, distant, now a stark description of my reality. One day, I found myself uttering a desperate plea, "This can't be my life." It wasn't a dramatic outburst; it was a quiet, chilling realization. I was trapped, frozen in a frame, a spectator in a life that felt alien. I was at a stalemate, a place where time ceased to flow, where emotions were muted, and where reality itself seemed to blur.

The universe, once a source of wonder and possibility, felt like it had abandoned me. I was deemed dissociated by my mental health team, a diagnosis that felt less like a label and more like a description of a state of being. It was the essence of being frozen, of existing in a liminal space where the present was a distant echo, and the future a hazy, unreachable horizon. It was a disconnect, a severing of the ties that bound me to the world, to myself.

My body, a battleground of neglect, mirrored the turmoil within. The physical symptoms I had been treating – the head injury, the chronic back pain, the twisted tailbone, the returning pre-diabetes, the leaking heart valve, the memory loss, the cognitive decline, the thyroid dysfunction – they were all intertwined with my mental state. The jury was still out on which came first, the mind or the body, but the treatments I sought, the attempts to patch the physical wounds, seemed only to exacerbate the underlying problems. I was treating the symptoms, not the disease, and the disease was a profound disconnect, a crippling dissociation.

I was dying in plain sight, a slow, agonizing unraveling. Depression and anxiety were my constant companions, whispering doubts and fears, amplifying the sense of isolation. I was trapped in a cycle of doing my best, of soldiering on, even as the circumstances grew increasingly dire. I was making excuses, justifying my neglect, perpetuating the downward spiral.

The breaking point arrived with a stark, physical manifestation of my inner paralysis. I remember throwing myself from my bed, a desperate attempt to break free from the invisible chains that bound me. I crawled towards my walking cane, a symbol of my physical and emotional fragility, desperate to regain some semblance of functionality. I looked around, pleading silently for a savior, a rescuer, a doctor, a psychologist, a social worker – anyone to pull me from the abyss. But the resolution, I was beginning to understand, was far more complex, far more internal.

By pressing forward, by ignoring my own needs, I had become my own architect of decline. The trajectory I was on was unsustainable, a path leading to complete and utter collapse. Even as I sought treatment – neurological surgery, partial thyroid removal, radiofrequency ablation, hypnosis, pain therapy – I was still trying to squeeze these crucial interventions into the margins of an already overflowing schedule. It was a fruitless attempt to repair the damage without addressing the root cause.

Then, a glimmer of hope. In the midst of my despair, my friends offered a new perspective: embrace "start" instead of "start over." I didn't need to erase my past, to reinvent myself. I needed to begin from where I was, to acknowledge the person I had become, to build upon the foundation of my experiences. I needed to stop trying to revive the old Federica and envision a new one, defined by her values, her goals, her evolved understanding of herself.

It's a cruel irony, isn't it? For over fifteen years, I've championed the mantra 'know where you stand and move forward' as the guiding principle of my small business. Yet, I, its founder, its very heart, failed utterly to apply that wisdom to my own life. I preached clarity, but lived in a fog. I urged forward motion, but remained mired in place, a testament to the chasm between my words and my actions. How could I, the very architect of this philosophy, become its most glaring contradiction?"

However, like Naaman in 2 Kings 5:1, I now understand that I don't need to be made better, I need to be made new. I need to shed the layers of trauma, the masks of pretense, the burdens of expectation. I need to embrace the vulnerability, the uncertainty, the raw, unfiltered truth of my existence. I need to step out of the frozen frame, to reclaim my narrative, to begin again, not from the beginning, but from the present, from the place of profound transformation.

The Thaw

"Wake up, shake it off", whispers something out there.

"You must respond to this pleading care".

But time stands still, in frozen pose,

Where life suspends, and nothing grows.

The mind a still, a stark before and after juxtapose,

Where thoughts congeal, and health undisposed.

"Wake up, shake it off", whispers something out there.

"You must respond to this pleading care".

A heart encased, where joy is denied

Where feelings grow numb, but fears reside.

No inner spark, no outward stride,

A frozen soul, where passions died.

"Wake up, shake it off", whispers something out there.

"You must respond to this pleading care".

The inner clock, has ceased its chime,

A frozen moment, lost to time.

To thaw a must, a sacred sign.

The shift is waiting, the destined climb.

Day 13

Embers of Hope

I've reached a day of nascent possibilities, gasping tentative breaths after a long, suffocating, frozen state. The future, once a distant, impossible landscape, now harbors a faint outline of a path forward, visible as the fog begins to lift, the darkness receding, revealing glimpses of light, of potential. But the path remains shrouded in a lingering haze, the questions pressing, urgent: What do I choose to do next? What will truly bring me peace? What should I do exactly? What is best for me? I've come to a profound realization: some of these answers are not mine to define. I am a child of God, and this arduous journey, this pending shift, has led me back to surrendering, to allowing Him to take the lead, to trust in a plan greater than my own.

Opportunities, I was slowly learning, often arrived in disguise, masquerading as mundane encounters, chance conversations, unexpected invitations. I had always been drawn to quick fixes, to immediate solutions, to the seductive illusion of control. But the crucible of the past years had forged a new understanding within me: healing was not a sprint, but a marathon, a journey, not a destination. It demanded long-term solutions, solutions that nurtured my spirit, that fed my soul, that allowed me to grow and evolve, to rebuild from the ashes of my former self.

And in the midst of my raw vulnerability, a series of serendipitous encounters unfolded, a constellation of positive people who seemed to appear as if orchestrated by a divine hand. They saw me, or at least, they saw the ember of light within me, even when I couldn't perceive it myself. It was as if the universe, having stripped me bare, was now offering me a lifeline, a series of guiding lights to illuminate my path, to lead me out of the darkness and into a future I could barely dare to dream of. These weren't mere coincidences; they were whispers of hope, tangible signs that I was not alone, that even in my brokenness, I was being held, guided, and gently nudged toward a new dawn.

The ordinary and routine, became a canvas for the extraordinary. A simple trip to the DMV, a place synonymous with waiting and paperwork, bloomed into a profound exchange of faith and hard-won wisdom. The woman behind the counter, her voice a balm to my weary spirit, shared her own troubled story, a clear brushstroke of divine grace. For a moment, suspended in time, the purpose of my visit dissolved, the building line a mere shadow, as a sense of something greater filled the space between us.

Divine Intervention?!

I remember a routine doctor's appointment, usually a sterile, clinical experience, morphed into a moment of unexpected spiritual connection. A nurse, sensing the unspoken depths of my pain, risked her job to offer a spontaneous prayer, a shared moment of devotion in both English and Spanish, a language that echoed the cultural roots of her own family. It was a moment of pure, unadulterated human connection, a tangible manifestation of divine presence.

Divine Intervention?!

Another nurse, with eyes that seemed to see beyond the surface, knew of my physical pain and procedures in their office, but sensed my unspoken longing for connection. She offered not just medical insight, but social engagement and support, a simple act of kindness that felt genuine. She still communicates with me although I am no longer a patient at her practice and still injects hope, empowerment and connection at the most opportune moments.

Divine Intervention?!

A seemingly random gig site booking delivered a handyman, a man going through eerily similar health struggles, bearing my father's very name. He possessed the same resourcefulness, the same knack for solving problems that others sought to exploit for extreme profit. Before my dad's passing, he was our family's cornerstone, our resident handyman, capable of tackling any project. He was the embodiment of 'can-do.' When I impulsively bought a vintage '63 Chevrolet Impala off eBay, and it was not quite like the pictures upon arrival, he brought it back to life, his hands working magic on its worn mechanics. When we needed new flooring to sell our house, he transformed the space with precision and care. When my cousin envisioned a new wing for her home, he built it, a testament to his skill and dedication. So you can understand the profound sense of divine intervention when this stranger, a white man bearing my father's name and spirit, appeared. It was as if a piece of my dad had been sent back to me, a reminder of the strength and support I thought I'd lost forever. He not only resolves the immediate practical problems, but also became a friend, a confidant, a reservoir of understanding in a time of profound despair. His presence is a gentle affirmation, a sign that I was not alone, that even in the midst of loss, I was being cared for.

Divine Intervention?!

One day during my sorrows, a friend and neighbor asked me to assist her while she worked as a vendor at an event after her help pulled out. My kids were away for the weekend so I joined her. As I sat at the vendor station I listened to the event- it was a women's empowerment luncheon.

I quickly realized that this sense of community was what I was missing to properly combat loneliness and despair. Since, the women of this faith-based organization have become my unwavering anchors. They aren't just casual acquaintances; they are a sisterhood, a circle of non-judgmental support. Their check-ins are more than polite inquiries; they are heartfelt expressions of genuine concern, a constant reminder that I am not alone in my struggles, and that I am invaluable and beautifully made. They offer more than just words; they offer practical assistance, a listening ear, and a shoulder to lean on. They are genuinely invested in my well-being, not as a fleeting gesture, but as a steadfast commitment. In a world that often feels cold and indifferent, they offer warmth, compassion, and a tangible sense of belonging. They pray with me, encourage me, and remind me of my inherent worth, even when I struggle to see it myself. The group allows opportunities to reciprocate and pour into the 'right' things. This group is a testament to the power of faith and the strength of female solidarity. Their presence in my life is a gentle reminder that even when life seems to unravel, there are still pockets of kindness, communities of support, and a genuine love for people abound.

Divine Intervention?!

One day, driven by a desperate need for focus and a return to productivity, I made the decision to seek an office space outside the confines of my home. I had heard of a co-working space nearby, envisioning it merely as a neutral location to work. Little did I know, this seemingly mundane decision was a pivotal moment, a divine orchestration. The space was run by women of strong faith, women whose very presence act as a powerful force to dispel the insidious tendrils of doubt and the crippling effects of imposter syndrome. It isn't just a place to work; it is a sanctuary, a haven where I found not just peers, but people I look up to. The leaders at my co-working space became my cheerleaders, creating a space of profound belonging, where my ideas are not just heard, but valued and celebrated. They offer events that are more than mere social gatherings; they are carefully curated opportunities to shatter the walls of my isolation, to gently nudge me back into the world, to reconnect with the vibrant nature of human connection. Heck, the color scheme of the office even matches my business branding also established over the last 15 years. It was as if a divine hand had guided me to this place, a place where I could begin to rebuild, to rediscover my purpose, and to find comfort in the company of kindred spirits.

Divine Intervention?!

These example encounters over the last year or so may seem like random and isolated events, as there are many more like these. I wholeheartedly believe they were not coincidences. It was God. It was God sending his broken and lost child reminders that even in the darkest of times, there is light, there is connection, there is possibility. This has led to the most substantial realization in my shift, the rediscovery of the power of faith. I realized that I had always relied on external sources, on my father's faith, on the familiar rhythms of church. I had never cultivated my own personal relationship with God. In my struggles, I had turned to every other solution, every other quick fix, every other external source. And I had failed.

But God! The phrase echoed in my mind, a testament to the power of surrender, of letting go, of trusting in a higher power. I had to intentionally turn towards faith, towards a personal connection with the divine to lead me in my process. As I make this shift, these glimmers of light have manifested and intensified, transforming into a radiant beam of optimism and hope.

I have entered into a process of sowing, of planting seeds of faith, of nurturing the hope within me. It is my recognition that healing isn't just about fixing what is broken; it is about cultivating what is whole, about nurturing the spirit, about embracing the possibility of transformation. It is a realization that even in the midst of chaos, even in the depths of despair, there is always the potential for growth, for renewal, for a future filled with light.

Among the voices that resonated deeply within my soul during my ongoing period of rediscovery is that of a pastor (also bearing my father's name) whose "I'm Proof" movement ignites a spark of defiant optimism. His most recent message, a challenge to strive to be the living embodiment of the impossible made possible, struck a chord within me. It isn't just about overcoming obstacles; it was about transforming them into a testament for others. My aim, I realize, is not simply to survive this season, but to emerge from it renewed, transformed, and empowered. I want to become the very evidence that challenges, no matter how overwhelming, are not the final chapter. I envision myself as a living testament to the power of faith, resilience, and the belief that there is indeed more on the other side – a future filled with purpose, joy, and the ability to inspire others to believe in their own capacity for transformation.

Sowing Seeds

The chains release,

        the grip unwinds,

A new journey starts,

        releasing time.

Quick fixes fade,

        a deeper quest sought,

For seeds of faith,

        and the lessons taught.

Serendipitous paths,

        uncover guiding light,

Kindred hearts,

        disrupt the plight.

Now the path reveals,

       a winding track,

Where broken pieces,

       can gather back.

Where the spirit soars,

       a liberated cry,

Where newfound strength,

       ascends the sky.

Where barren ground,

       yields a blossom's grace,

She cements her place,

       in God's embrace.

Day 14

Embracing the Shift

This is not an ending, but a beginning. A transformation. A becoming. A day of clarity, of resolve, of stepping into the seedling that had sprouted, then flourished, within me. This journey, these fourteen days, have been a reckoning, a dismantling, and a rebuilding. A confrontation with the past, an exploration of the present, and a deliberate, intentional shaping of the future.

I stand at the threshold, looking back at the woman I was, the woman I had allowed myself to become. The woman defined by roles, by expectations, by the shadows of trauma and the weight of societal pressures. I was more than just a "tool" to be used, a token, someone's mom or wife. I was a force, a spirit, a being of limitless potential, waiting to be unleashed. I was not a pendulum, swinging back and forth between extremes, between victim and victor. This life, I realized, wasn't a series of reactive swings, but a deliberate, conscious journey of creation.

"Shifted." What does it mean? It's more than a change, more than a simple adjustment. It's a fundamental transformation, a seismic shift in perspective, in identity, in purpose. It's the shedding of old skins, the release of limiting beliefs, the embrace of authentic self. It's the transition from surviving to thriving, from existing to living, from being defined by external forces to defining my own reality. It's the realization that I am not a product of my circumstances, but a creator of my destiny.

"Shifted" is the embodiment of resilience, the tangible proof that even in the face of overwhelming adversity, transformation is possible. It's the journey of moving from invisibility to visibility, from silence to voice, from brokenness to wholeness. It is about understanding that the scars we carry are not signs of weakness, but symbols of strength, testaments to our ability to endure, to overcome, to rise.

In the context of this book, "Shifted" is the journey you've witnessed, a raw and unfiltered exploration of my inner landscape, a testament to the power of vulnerability and the courage to confront the shadows of the past. But "Shifted" is not confined to these pages. It's a call to action, an invitation to embark on your own journey of transformation. It's a reminder that you, too, have the power to redefine your narrative, to rewrite your story, to become the person you were always meant to be.

Beyond the pages of this book, "Shifted" is a way of life, a commitment to authenticity, a dedication to growth, a celebration of resilience. It's about living with intention, with purpose, with joy. It's about embracing the present moment, while simultaneously building a future that aligns with your deepest values and aspirations. It's about recognizing the interconnectedness of all things, the ripple effect of our actions, the power of our choices to shape not only our own lives, but the lives of those around us.

I am no longer content to be a spark of potential. I aim to be a wildfire of change, a testament to the power of transformation. I will be the proof that the impossible is possible, that even in the darkest of nights, light can prevail. I will embody the evidence that a fulfilling future exists beyond hardship, a future brimming with purpose, joy, and the power to ignite belief in others' transformative potential.

This is not the end of my journey, but a new beginning. I am "Shifted," and I am ready to embrace the future, to live a life of authenticity, purpose, and hope. And I invite you, dear reader, to join me. To embark on your own journey of transformation, to become the "Shifted" version of yourself, to shine your light brightly, and to create a world filled with hope, resilience, and boundless possibility.

Beaming

No fleeting whims, but a steady quest,

The moment has come, at God's behest.

Not crafted form, nor borrowed art,

But spirit's core, at its embryonic start.

"Shifted" whispers, a potent call,

To rise transformed, and give her all.

Authenticity's trail, a new journey's birth,

"Shifted" from fractured pieces, a renewed worth.

Resilience forged, a testament's claim,

To embrace her purpose with passion, and a restored frame.

The beam unfurls, such a radiant sight,

She's "Shifted" and whole, in boundless light.

www.ingramcontent.com/pod-product-compliance
Lightning Source LLC
Chambersburg PA
CBHW051232120626
46547CB00013B/1602